I0473515

Life Dances
Stories from the Indianapolis JCC and the
Albert and Sara Reuben Senior and Community
Resource Center
2014

INwords

Life Dances:
Stories from the Indianapolis JCC and the
Albert and Sara Reuben Senior and Community
Resource Center

Edited by Barbara Shoup, Michael Baumann, and
Andrea Boucher

Cover design by Andrea Boucher

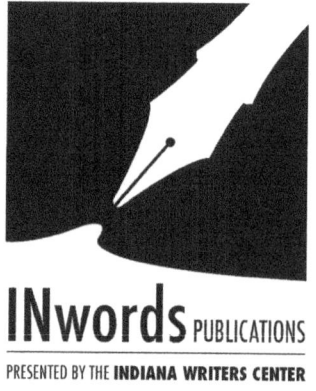

INwords PUBLICATIONS

PRESENTED BY THE **INDIANA WRITERS CENTER**

Published by INwords: Indianapolis, IN

ISBN: 978-0-9849501-5-7

© 2014 INwords / Indiana Writers Center. All
Rights Reserved.

Life Dances
Stories from the Indianapolis JCC and the
Albert and Sara Reuben Senior and Community
Resource Center

Edited by Barbara Shoup, Michael Baumann, and
Andrea Boucher

INwords Publications
PO Box 30407
Indianapolis, IN 46230-0407

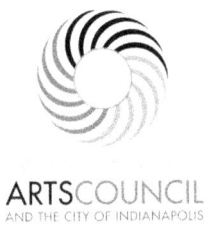

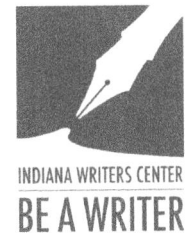

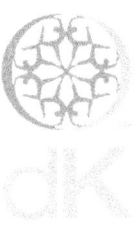

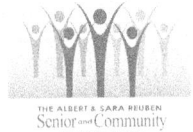

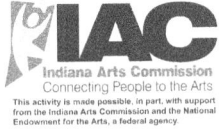

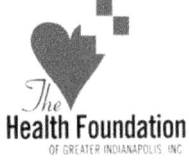

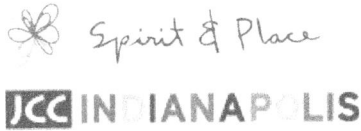

Contents

Introduction

1.
Life

On a brisk morning in early April, seniors from the JCC and the Albert & Sara Reuben Senior and Community Resource Center gather at round tables in the auditorium to write about their lives. Some are afraid their lives are too ordinary to be interesting; others have had life experiences so tragic and profound that they're afraid there are no words to describe them. Most haven't written anything but lists and the occasional letter since their school years and can't imagine how they will actually write a story good enough to be published in a book.

No worries, I tell them.

Every life is full of stories. Every story is worthy of being told.

Volunteers from the Indiana Writers Center are here to help you get them on the page.

And we begin.

First, I say, Write "I remember" followed by whatever comes into your head. Keep doing that until the timer goes off. Write "I remember" each time—and just a sentence or phrase. Your brain likes that rhythm. The memories that float up will be random, sometimes surprising. That's the way it's supposed to happen.

Most get a list of 10 or more in a few minutes, each one a snapshot of a real moment in time, a tiny first draft. Now pick one of the memories and do the exercise again, I say, writing "I remember" to dredge up details about that particular experience.

Now close your eyes, *see* the scene of your memory directly in front of you in your mind's eye. Look right, look left. Look above you, look below. Look behind you. What do you hear, smell, touch, taste?

Now write the story of what happens in your memory. Don't worry about grammar, spelling, organization or getting the right word. Just write. As fast as you can. All those things can be fixed later.

And they do. Heads bent, scribbling madly, they enter the world of the past.

They're at the L.S. Ayres Tea Room, ordering a princess sundae, they're meeting nice Jewish boys at a summer resort; they're on their way to school on the last trolley in New York City. They remember V-mail with words blacked out, telegrams with bad news, happy homecomings. First dates, weddings, the birth of children. Scaling the fence of a closed cemetery in Germany, determined to visit a father's grave.

They remember the sound of American bombers hitting the factories and train tracks in Gyor, the day the Nazis surrounded their labor camp, entering a ghetto in Hungary, where Hungarian Nazis rode bicycles and motorcycles, brandishing axes and knives. They remember wearing an armband with a yellow star. They remember wandering Europe when the war was over.

They remember people they loved and lost and, just for a moment, bring them back in words.

2.
Dances

In August, ten writers meet the members of Dance Kaleidoscope who have chosen to interpret their pieces in dance. It's a little awkward at first, but soon the room is filled with spirited conversation and occasional bursts of laughter. Writers beam as the dancers tell them why they chose their pieces and why, exactly, they love them. Dancers listen intently as writers answer the questions they've asked, filling in background, giving them a better, deeper understanding of the stories and the seniors who wrote them. Writers are curious to know how the dancers will turn words into dance.

The choreography will not be a literal interpretation of the story, they explain. Looking for strong words and phrases that capture the essence of the stories will be the first part of the creative process. Then they will experiment with gestures that carry emotion and information, developing them into phrases of movement that create a through line from one idea to the next, the overall impression resonating against the big picture of the story.

Music will enhance the mood of the piece. Personal photos and memorabilia will be cast on a screen behind the dancers, deepening the effect. Seniors may read their pieces aloud on the night of the performance, or have them read by a member of DK.

Over the next months, words will morph to movement and the joys and heartbreaks of individual lives will burst from the page into marvelous, visual stories. The DK performance will be a part of the JCC's Ann Katz Festival of Books and Arts and Indianapolis Spirit & Place in November.

When the curtain goes up, these ten stories will meet an appreciative audience.

All of the stories from the April workshop are collected in this anthology, which will delight readers for years to come.

Barbara Shoup
Executive Director
Indiana Writers Center

Life Dances
Collected Writing

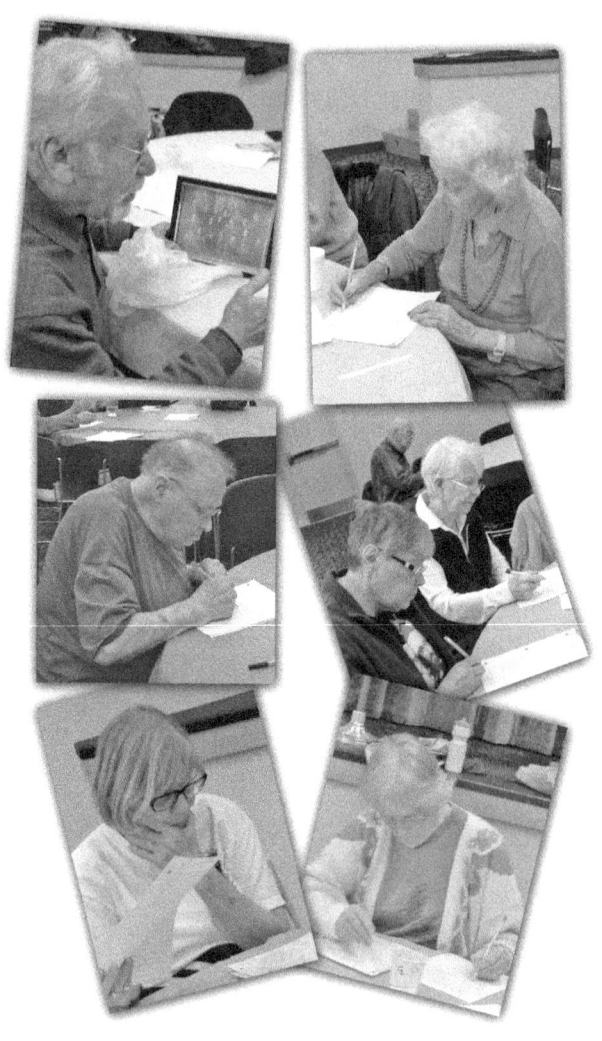

Rachel Albert

I remember a snowy day in December 1940. My mother crying, neighbors crying, everyone sad. I was left behind as my family all went away. I was confused, not knowing what was happening. Later that day I was told my father had died and that it was the day of his funeral.

I was five years old, the youngest of six children. My mother spoke little English. She was sad, worried, and overwhelmed.

My sister took my hand and put my hair in Shirley Temple curls. That made me feel happy again.

I remember during WWII my mother pacing the street waiting for the mailman. I had two brothers in the war. I was seven or eight at the time. I remember the letters sent home with spaces where the words were taken out—Victory Mail.

Sandra Marek Behringer

My mother's oldest brother, Matthew Glogowski, was captured at the Battle of the Bulge sometime between December 1944 and January 1945. At that time I was a child of seven. I recall the day a telegram came to my grandparents' home on Halsted Street in Harvey, Illinois, a suburb south of Chicago. It informed us that my Uncle Matt was missing in action. The family was devastated, and my grandma Josephine wept and cried, alternately shattered by her son's death and filled with fury at those she was certain had taken his life. Her anxiety for her three other sons, also soldiers, was beyond words, and she could not be comforted. So it was with an unbelievable sense of relief and hope that the family received a second telegram, sent many weeks later, that changed his status to that of a prisoner of war!

This story has a happy ending because sometime after May 1945, when the war in Europe was over, my thin, ill, but very much alive uncle returned to us. He would not talk about his experience in the camp but he did bring home a story and a souvenir.

He told us that when it was clear that his unit would be captured, from where he stood in a field he threw away, as far as he could, his mother's wedding ring, which she had given him as a token of her love and prayers for his protection. He said he could not bear the thought that a German soldier would take it from him and give it to a woman as spoils of war. My uncle's souvenir was a German luger, which Grandma pulled from his hands and, raising one of

the plates on her wood-burning stove, threw into the
fire, saying she would have no instrument of the
devil in her house.

Many years later, remembering this incident, I wrote
the poem, "HELEN—1945," which was my refusal
to forget those sad yet triumphant days for our
family. It was also written in homage to a time in my
childhood that cost so much in love and suffering
and grief to so many families.

HELEN
1945

The porch flickers grey
and peeling in the lightning
and the swing moves
into flashes of light and dark
past a window holding a banner
of four stars.

Not long ago Ma and I
would sit on the swing
peeling apples in a bowl.
She'd sing to me her songs
of Poland and Pa would wink
and push the swing too hard
and when she scolded, he'd stop
the thing on its upward flight
and kiss me.

Before they were stars
my uncles loved horses

and read Zane Grey into the night,
but since the yellow telegram
Billy's missing and our mailbox
is an empty mouth of pain
sucking our hearts dry.

Ma's stopped baking
and listens for their voices
in her head. Pa says
she'll be all right when they
come home but I'm afraid
they won't and mostly
he forgets to kiss me.

Oh, God, I am like this storm.
I want to scream like thunder
and smash against the window
like the rain. I want
thin air mail letters to fall
from the mailbox like the fear
from my mouth when I wake up
at night and hide in the bathroom
so they won't see.

I want to ride higher and higher
on this wooden swing, singing to them
until the lightning burns away the night,
until there are no stars, until I wake them
from their bad dreams.

Marilyn Block

I remember when I was growing up that my little sister could not pronounce my name. She called me "Lolly," like lollipop.

I remember going to California on the train. It took about five or six days to get to our destination. I remember our beds were berths, upper and lower. We ate in the dining room. The table was shaking back and forth. It was an experience I will never forget.

My father owned a men's clothing store. Every Monday after school, I waited for the bus to go downtown and meet my mother at Sonnefelds, a women's clothing store. We would go shopping. When my father closed up the store, we had dinner. My father's favorite meal was liver and onions. After dinner we headed home. PS., My mother always bought a split lemon cake at the bakery located in the restaurant.

My family went to California to a wedding when I was a flower girl. We went on a train, stopped in Denver. My father left his hat on a bench. My mother and I went to a department store and were locked into the store. We banged on the door and the janitor let us out. What a relief!

I remember when my twins were born. They came so soon, I barely made it to the hospital. They came six minutes apart. I heard one crying after birth, then the doctor knocked me out and the other was born. Twin boys.

I remember when I started going to the JCC. It took me a while to participate since I am not Esther Williams. Oh well, who cares? I'm doing it to help my bones and have been doing it ever since and enjoy it very much.

I am so happy belonging to the Rubin Center, meeting many nice people, going on trips—it is an education.

Lillian Bradley

I remember an area on West 21st and Boulevard Place. The large area on the west side was used for a carnival. Those carnivals had side shows, like the place with mirrors where you had to find your way out. There was music, clowns, and lots of side shows. I passed that area recently, and the area now is full of big factory buildings and not the fun place I remember.

Peg Bresko

I remember my husband and I were out in the back yard in Louisiana when I saw a black snake. My husband picked me up and as we were going back to the house, our hostess was spinning the chickens until their heads fell off. Ugh!! We were staying at her house during the war.

Meyer Bronicki

I remember …

… when the Nazis surrounded our labor camp.

… when I escaped from the labor camp.

… when I got to the Ozerany Village and they told us we were not welcome to stay and hide because we were Jews and too dangerous.

When I got married to Shoshana, I was happy. I got married during *Sfera*, the time between *Pesach* and *Lag ba'omer*, in June 1958. I wore a dark colored suit. Shoshana wore a Chinese style dress that was red with flowers. We got married in a temple in Tel Aviv. Shoshana took a ritual *mikvah* bath. Both Shoshana and I had relatives at our wedding. Her parents were there and so was her brother. I was overjoyed that people from my hometown attended our wedding. We had about 20 guests in all. I have really great memories of kissing Shoshana that day. *We were alive.* After the ceremony we went back to our home in *Petatikva* and played music and ate traditional Israeli food.

Dee Calderon

I remember living in a house with no plumbing or heating. I remember having pets. I remember first grade. I remember our trip to Washington, D.C., and Niagara Falls. I remember the ice man. I remember my grandparents. I remember the grape vines and wine barrels. I remember my first bike. I remember taking baths in the washtub. I remember my mother making my clothes and sewing quilts.

I remember the chickens we raised. One banty rooster was really mean. It chased me one day, and I did not want to lose the battle.

I remember the wine barrels and the grape vines, my father making wine during the 1930s. I was told to stay away from the barrel. On a beautiful summer day, my father's wine barrel with homemade wine was just sitting there. I know, stay away. The grape vines were getting low on grapes. The chickens were being chased by the banty rooster, that mean critter. I needed to teach him a lesson. What an afternoon! I did not think I would ever catch him—but I did! Now what? I know—off to the wine barrel we went. I dropped him into the barrel. I don't know if he drowned or got drunk!

Betty Carlin

I remember South Haven, Michigan, a wonderful place to be a teenage Jewish girl. More boys, all Jewish and working in the hotels—what fun! Beach fires and singing at night. The boys were all there to earn money to go back to college in the fall. Since they were all Jewish, the girls' mothers thought they were okay for their daughters to date. South Haven was a wonderful place to be a Jewish teenage girl. The same boys returned to work there every year. We had such fun around the fire each evening—my girlfriends loved to visit me. The boys often showed off their athletic prowess by standing on each other's shoulders or making pyramids together balancing on the sand. I went home with fond memories and pictures to show the girls back home! What fun. Since everyone was Jewish, we had common ideas. Mothers thought since everyone was Jewish, they had to be good! My summer home called Ariel was a popular place for friends to visit in the summer. When the boys stood under my window to call me to the beach, my sister Margie (5 ½ years younger) would shout out "We'll be right down!" And she went. Apple Annie walked the beach barefoot in the hot sand carrying her tray of caramel apples over her head with both hands. We must have paid a quarter! When I think about caramel apples today, I think about my toes in the sand. The same friends came back year after year. A great place to be a teenage girl! My house was a popular spot. The bonfires, the beach at night are still beautiful memories.

Rita Casey

We called Yonkers the next-to-the-largest-city in the world because it was next to New York City. I lived in Woodlawn, in the Bronx. The last trolley in NYC went from the end of the line on Jerome Avenue in the Bronx to the center of Yonkers and dropped me off at Seton Academy for Young Ladies. The trolley took me along Van Cortlandt Park, where we ice skated on the lake in "Vanny." I learned to ski on the hills right there in the Bronx! This trolley also went past the Woodlawn Cemetery, one of the largest with many famous people buried there. The trolley started next to a horse barn, where I took riding lessons. We trotted under the el and over the trolley tracks to ride the trails in beautiful Vanny. A driving school sat next to the barn. I learned to drive around the el pillars and the trolley.

I was a junior in high school and Maurice (Moe) Casey was a freshman at Fordham College waiting to go into the Naval Air Corps. In those days, many of the Catholic Churches in NYC had dances in their auditoriums one night a week with a DJ and records. It was the Big Band Era. My church had theirs every Friday night. This is where we met, doing the Lindy Hop to Glenn Miller, Harry James, Benny Goodman, Duke Ellington, and the Dorsey Brothers. Moe was a terrific dancer. "String of Pearls," "Pennsylvania 6-5000," "Sentimental Journey," and "Dancing in the Dark" were some of our favorites. Years later "It Had to Be You" was "our song." He went off to WWII while I finished high school and enrolled in the College of New Rochelle. Thank God the war ended just before his aircraft carrier left San Diego for Japan. He returned to Fordham University. This time, I was a year ahead of him. We danced our way through college, and in my junior year we became engaged. On August 9, 1949, two months after my graduation, we were married at Saint Barnabas Church and had a fun reception eating and dancing at the Tavern on the Green in Central Park.

We flew to Bermuda and after two wonderful weeks cruised home on the Queen of Bermuda. He went back to college and I taught sixth grade in the Bronx. My students were adorable and loved me because I was young and not in a nun's habit. I taught only one semester because I got pregnant and couldn't teach in that condition. Luckily the Telephone Company was hiring. I talked to customers on the phone, and they couldn't see my expanding tummy. I made $2.50 more a week than I made as a teacher. I worked right up until a week before Moe's graduation in June, 1950. I had Tommy, the first of our fabulous eight children a month later on the Fourth of July (he was our firecracker). Moe got a job with National Cash Register Company two days after graduation and worked for them for almost 40 years. He retired as Regional Manager of Major Retail Accounts for the Northeast Region of NCR in 1988. We had a great sixty-four years dancing every chance we could get—at dances, parties, and most recently, our grandchildren's weddings.

Eleanor Cohen

The Ticket

In 1960, my maternal grandmother, Leah, was dying.
I was living in Detroit at the time, flying into
Indianapolis every three weeks with my two-year-old
daughter to see her. By some fluke of nature, for five
generations in my mother's family, even the cousins,
each family produced only one daughter. No girl in
our family had a sister. In every case, the parents
lived next door to, or with, that daughter. She was
the one who provided love, care, and
companionship over the years. The bond between
mother and daughter was extremely strong. My
mother and grandmother would cook together and
talk and I would be there listening to all their stories.

When my grandmother married at the age of sixteen,
she moved far away from St. Petersburg to a small
farm ten miles from the German border. There lived
a 19-year-old sister-in-law. They became fast, loving
friends. They both became pregnant. My 17-year-old
great grandmother was the only person in attendance
when the sister-in-law gave birth to a breech baby,
nearly dying in the process. Leah could do nothing
but stand there and cry.

One day when my grandfather was working in the
fields, the Cossacks came riding through and
grabbed him and a number of other men and
marched them for miles and miles in circles and
circles so that they would get lost and not be able to
run away and go back home. Similarly, the men were

16

never told who the enemy was or what country they were in. The families, of course, knew nothing. If a battle was close by, the woman would go to the battlefield to look at the dead or wounded to see if their husband or son was among them.

After a few years away, the army made the mistake of giving my grandfather a furlough. As soon as she saw him, my grandmother took her dowry to town, sold it, and gave my grandfather the money to buy a ticket to America. He went to the ticket office and said the one word in English that he knew, "America." They sold him a ticket. To South America.

Eventually, he ended up in New York from whence he sent for the rest of the family. Letters between the sisters-in-law were frequent. During the early 1930s, there was disturbing news about the treatment of Jews in Germany. Because the family took their produce to sell right at the German border, they heard directly from the Jews involved. My grandmother wrote reassuring letters in reply. "Don't worry about the Germans. They are the most civilized country in Europe. Consider their universities, their music, literature, science, and general level of education. Even if there is a war, why worry? We are only poor farmers. Why would they ever bother with us? We survived WWI, we will survive this, too."

The worried letters continued. The last one said that the family had held a meeting. They said they realized she could not bring them all over, so they selected one of their number to receive a ticket. They picked the sister-in-law as the person most likely to be able to succeed in America. She had what they referred to as "golden hands." She could create beautiful, complicated dresses without a pattern, create beautiful works of embroidery and lace and cook delicious food. Please send her a ticket.

My grandmother didn't. It was the Depression. Money was short. She procrastinated, the war started, and then she couldn't. She never received another letter. When I last saw my grandmother, she was walking in circles around the living room, wringing her hands and crying, "Forgive me. Forgive me. Please, please forgive me." I asked her why. She said it was her fault her sister-in-law had died. I said it wasn't. It was the Nazis who had killed her. She said no. She hadn't sent her the ticket.

It is the custom among my people to name a new baby for someone in the family whom you respect and whose memory you wish to perpetuate. As long as the name is spoken, that person will live on in memory.

There had been babies born to us over the years. I asked Grandma why we had not given one that name. A look of the most terrible, indescribable pain crossed her face. And then I understood why. Every time the child was called, every time her name was mentioned, that overwhelming pain and guilt would recur. It was too heavy a burden to bear. I asked Grandma what the name was. She barely whispered, and I almost didn't hear it. "Hannah Leah."

All right, Hannah Leah. I have told your story. My teenage grandson has promised me that when he grows up, marries and has a daughter, he will name

18

her Hannah Leah. I know he will. And you, Hannah Leah, will be remembered.

When I was a student at Indiana University, my art teacher gave us the assignment to draw something from an unusual perspective. I took my drawing pad outside and started wandering about. It was a beautiful spring day. I came across a deserted construction site. It was noon, so there was not a worker in sight. I saw a big tall crane with a big bucket on the end. I thought the top of that crane would be a good place for me to park while making a picture. The crane had big bolts that stuck out about an inch on each side. I thought they would make a handy ladder to climb up to the top, so I did. I made my drawings and threw the pad to the ground, where it plopped into some rising dust. I started back down and came to a horrible realization. Climbing up was easy. I could see each bolt. But coming down I couldn't see a thing, and I would have to feel for each bolt with my foot. If I missed, I would have a nasty fall, hitting each protruding bolt on the way. I looked down. Ten feet is a long way up. I thought, now I know what a treed cat must feel like. I decided I would have to jump. A gray hill was close by and I aimed for that. I jumped, and to my horror I saw my legs and feet disappear into the hill. The hill was made of ashes, and they were puffing up all around me. I closed my eyes and held my breath. I figured if I didn't panic and just walked in a straight line, I wouldn't suffocate.

Obviously, I made it out. I came back to the dormitory completely covered in ashes. No one said a word. I was an art major and they were used to me.

Frieda (Bunny) Cohen

I remember how I was named Bunny. I had a toy bunny and my sister couldn't say my name, so she called me Bunny. Now I am 92 years old and everyone still calls me Bunny.

I remember when I married my first husband. He was a soldier, and we got married at the Claypool Hotel. He was sent to South Carolina and would not let me come there because it was a terrible place! Then he went overseas and was gone a year. I did not hear from him for a long time. The Red Cross finally found him, and he was still overseas.

I remember growing up with my parents, four sisters, and one brother. To this day, I hate living alone.

I remember living over our department store. When my parents knocked on the pipes, we knew to go down to the store and help. One day a man came into the store and held up my father, yelling and pointing a gun at him. A little fox terrier puppy ran to the man and bit him. My father was able to get into the door of our apartment.

Another time a fellow stole jackets and ran. My brother-in-law Charles Caplin ran after him, and the guy turned on him and shot him. Thank God he survived.

The only time the department store closed was on Jewish holidays. The people who were not Jewish appreciated this. One side of Roosevelt Avenue (where the store was located) was white and the other side black. We all got along well.

During the Depression, my sister Neoma said we were poor but we didn't realize we were poor because we always had food and clothes.

Toba Cohen

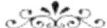

In 1969, my husband and I decided to take a trip to Israel with our friends, two other couples. Since we had not traveled outside the US, we needed to apply for passports. The first step was to provide a birth certificate, which neither of us had. At that time we needed to go the office that issued the certificates. I gave them my maiden name, Toba Epstein, saying I was born at Methodist Hospital on September 6, 1926. "Sorry, we have no record." So after searching, they found a Thema Epstein. So I learned that after my parents named me Thema, my grandfather changed my name to Toba in memory of his grandmother.

Joanna Day

Adrienne called. She had a lump on her collarbone and was going for a biopsy. She was 23. She was in Oregon. We were leaving for Toronto on a trip the next morning. Allan and I were going to cancel our trip and go to Oregon. She said, "No, go on your trip. It is probably nothing. I will have the doctor call you after the procedure."

Our friends Jim and Janet came to spend the evening with us since our only daughter could have cancer. They drove to Toronto and spent the weekend with us. Monday I went to work and waited and waited for the doctor to call. No call. I stayed late at work and still no call. Finally I drove home. Allan met me at the door of the garage when I pulled in and parked the car. I asked if the doctor had called. He didn't answer. I asked again, "Did the doctor call?" Again he didn't answer. I asked the third time and my husband turned to me with tears in his eyes. "Adrienne has cancer."

That night we cried in each other's arms. Our only daughter had cancer. Our only son had MS. What was the worth of all our hard work, what was the worth of anything, when our children both had life-threatening diseases?

The next morning we boarded a plane for Portland, Oregon. I cried all the way across the country, and I prayed and I prayed. I prayed to be able to stop the tears. I didn't want her to see that this was the end of the world. I wanted her to have hope.

Joe Frankovitz

I remember when a salesperson knocked on the front door wanting to sell something to Mother. When she said she didn't want to buy anything, he called her a foreigner and cussed her out. I remember that my mother cried because of what the man said.

My mother came to America when she married my dad. They were cousins to one another. I can remember when my father was overseas and when my mother was aware that a bully by the name of Mike Beard used to beat up on us kids. The bully had an accident and fell from his bike onto the street pavement. I remember that she left our house and ran out to the bully. She helped him up and got him onto our front porch so he could sit down. I also remember that the bully was a lot nicer to me and stopped picking on me.

I remember when I first rode a bike—a Western Flyer Bike. I was nine to eleven years old.

I remember the very first large tree I climbed.

I remember the first roof I jumped off.

I remember my first fight.

Marion Simon Garmel

I remember Sunday lunches with my aunts and uncles at our house. My mother would fry chicken in a big electric skillet. The aunts and uncles would be around in the den awaiting the call to dinner and two of them, my Aunt Lena and my Uncle Sidney, each had one shot of scotch before dinner. Since Aunt Lena, we later learned, had been and probably still was an alcoholic, that must have been torture.

The call would come and we all moved to the dining room table where the finest fried chicken in all of El Paso, TX was served. With mashed potatoes and gravy, green beans, salad with guacamole and salsa. A lunch of Tex-Mex Sunday dinner.

I remember traveling to California when I was about 10 and my sister was 8. We traveled alone on the Sunset Limited from El Paso to Los Angeles, where we would meet our father, a traveling salesman.

The train was our playground and we raced from car to car. We spent a lot of time in the bar car where a gentleman tried to teach us how to do card tricks.

In Beverly Hills, Dad took us to lunch at the Beverly Hills Hotel. Then we got in the car and drove around the hot desert, stopping in Calexico, California, the hottest town I had ever been in. We splashed in the pool at the hotel. California is still my favorite place in America.

Margaret Glesing

I.

The long weekend trip sponsored by WFYI (Channel 20) is an especially treasured memory. PBS televised the Boston Pops with Arthur Fiedler, and that was the centerpiece for the trip. But there was so much more! Accommodations were in a hotel on Copley Square with historic sights. (The Boston Public Library and a stupendous church building were right there.) We walked downtown to pick up the Freedom Trail. What an exhilarating and thought-provoking American history lesson. Quincy Market was such fun—so many exotic foods new to my Midwestern experience, especially the fish.

The walk back—uphill all the way—took us past the swan boats in action. It was hard to resist taking a ride. A walk into the adjoining neighborhood was a different cultural experience. Breakfast coffee with lots of milk. That was not the way to drink coffee.

Then there was the concert. We weren't at one of those cute snack tables, but we enjoyed the glorious music just as well in a regular seat at a site we had seen so often on PBS—all dressed up in our concert clothes.

But there was more. The afternoon we spent at an authentic New England lobster boil. Another culture difference. Messy, but oh, so yummy! Especially waterside, with all the intriguing sounds and smells.

Thank you, Channel 20!

II.

Grandfather took me to visit cousins, aunts, and uncles in the Wisconsin countryside. This was a big culture change for me because I was a city girl. I got to collect chicken eggs, work in the garden, and milk cows. It was a world of outhouses, oil lamps, fresh food, peas in the pod, and no TV! I don't remember what we did in the evenings

I remember my dad helping me learn to ride a bike.

I remember going ice-skating on the Milwaukee River.

I remember going downtown to see my first movie.

Clara Gordon

43 Patton Avenue N.E. is the address of the house I was born in in Roanoke, Virginia, the "Star City of the South." It's called this because there is a very large electrical star that sits on the top of Mill Mountain. It is one of the largest man-made electric stars in the U.S.A.

The mountain is a friendly and easy to climb mountain. My neighborhood friends and I would climb it and walk around the gigantic star as we tried to figure out how many lights it took to make the star visible all around our hometown.

I lived there for eight years. Our home was a comfortable two-story, three-bedroom house that was painted gray, and sat on a little hill. The house was just right for our family: Mother, Daddy, Norman Grant, and me: Clara Thurman. My older brother had died as a new baby, but I never knew why he died. My mother often spoke of the baby, Jack Alexander. "He was such a beautiful baby," Mother said. "He was gorgeous and had coal black straight hair." I think she must have memorized his physical body during the one day that he lived.

I was named Clara for my mother and Thurman for my grandmother, Blanch Thurman, who was married to my grandfather, Abner Hurt. My Uncle Willie lived into his eighties, and he always loved me. He was married to a very pretty lady named Mae, and they had one son named Bobbie. He moved to

New York with his mother after she divorced Uncle Willie. Afterwards, Uncle Willie met another pretty lady, who was a gambler. Her name was Christine, and she wore many diamond rings. She was a fantastic card player. She gambled with men who worked for the Norfolk and Western Railroad. They would get off their jobs on the passenger trains and head straight to Uncle Willie and Aunt Christine's house. The men's pockets were loaded with money and Willie and Christine were ready.

Their house looked like a museum. It was furnished with gorgeous antiques, oriental rugs, crystal, silver, and the most expensive furniture you could purchase. All of my Mother's siblings had beautiful homes that were furnished with antiques and fine furniture. I was amazed at how similar their homes appeared to me. Their taste was so similar.

Two of Mother's sisters had worked for a very wealthy white lady who was the president of a fine college for rich white young ladies. I was privileged several times to go with my aunts to visit this dynamic woman. One of my visits is still ingrained in my memory. I remember being directed into the large house and through the long hallway to the stairs and then to a bedroom that was larger than any bedroom I had ever seen. The bed and the other furniture appeared to be gigantic. I remember being further impressed with the foot stools that provided a lift to the person who had to get into the bed.

As I grew into my early teens, it became quite clear to me that skin color was an issue. For example, my aunts who worked for the lady president were very light-skinned/white. My mother, Uncle Willie, Aunt

Berta, and Aunt Minnie were brown-skinned people, like my brother and me. I thank God that my aunts and uncles on both sides, Mother's and Daddy's, were elegant, classy looking, beautiful people. And they ranged in color from light/white to dark-brown-skinned. My grandfather, Abner Hurt, was white-skinned with blue eyes and reddish hair. His wife, my mother's mother, Blanch Thurman, was brown-skinned with long straight black hair. She looked like she was from the Potawatomi tribe. Growing up in segregated Virginia was easy for me, as well as I remember. We "colored people" lived in the northeast, northwest and southwest in town. The white people lived in South Roanoke, on the "other side" of town. I did not know any white children, nor do I remember seeing any. In addition, I do not have any memory of seeing their schools, churches, parks, etc. However, by the time I was six years old, I knew where most of our African American, "colored," churches and schools and neighborhoods were.

One family that interested me very much was the Claytons. They had a large house right across from the street from our First Baptist Church. They did not attend our church, but instead they were Episcopalians. I never went to their church, but I do remember Mother mentioning that all of the "colored" people who went to that church looked and sometimes passed for white. I suppose this was comfortable for them when they traveled outside the Southern states of America.

Passing was a very commonplace activity for some of my parents' friends, as it might have been for Papa, my mother's father, who had the beautiful eyes. None of my aunts or uncles inherited Papa's blue eyes, but several of us grandchildren have green eyes and sandy-colored hair.

This was a big disadvantage for me because I attended Gainsborough Elementary School, where no other child looked like me. I was beaten up every day and I had no idea why the other girls pulled the bows of my hair ribbon. They made me cry every day. I do not remember every having one teacher help me during the confrontations. Finally, after many tears and loosened bows of ribbon on my hair, my parents decided to move me to Harrison Avenue School, which was father away but much nicer. I was no big deal there. I felt comfortable and I enjoyed the new lifestyle of having kids play with me during recess rather than beat me up and make me cry.

From Harrison Avenue School I moved into Booker T. Washington Junior High. Wow! This was great! We changed classes, went to lunch and playgrounds without a teacher to oversee us, and we could stop off at the neighborhood restaurant after school. I would have brought enough money to purchase a hotdog and a soda before walking the rest of the way home.

Mr. Powell was my science teacher and he was great! He moved into a neighbor lady schoolteacher's house, a few houses away from mine. I really *liked* this young man and he became sort of a friend. He let me drive his new Chevrolet in our school parade and he always smiled warmly at me. Today I am so grateful to God and thankful to Mr. Powell for being a gentleman, a wonderful teacher and a friend to me. I thank him for understanding that I had a crush on him, but I was only a child. Later, he was transferred to Lucy Addison High School, where he was my science teacher again. At last! I graduated from high school and was ready for college at seventeen years old. 1958. So off to Hampton Institute I went in Hampton, Virginia, the Tidewater area of the South. We freshmen had to wear green beanies and braided hair, and we had to speak to all upper class students each time we saw them.

By this time, the Civil Rights Movement was well underway and the predominately Black colleges were becoming involved. There was a gentleman named Martin Luther King, Jr. who was speaking out about civil rights, and his words, speeches and voice were being heard in the South. I was attending Ebenezer Baptist Church and Reverend Jeep Smith wanted to get our church and community involved. Dr. Martin Luther King was invited to come and speak to our congregation. He accepted. We held the meeting and there were three people in attendance: Clara Thurman Carter, Rev. Jeep Smith, and Dr. Martin Luther King, Jr. Jeep Smith and I were deeply impressed with Dr. King, and we started holding meetings in churches in and around Virginia. That one meeting I attended to greet, meet, and learn from Dr. King changed my life entirely.

After graduating from Hampton Institute, now Hampton College, I applied to Columbia University. I was accepted, attended, and received my Master of Arts degree. While in New York, I met a young man named Michael V.W. Gordon, who lived and taught school in Manhattan, East Harlem. Later we became engaged and were married in an all-white Episcopal Church in Roanoke. We lived in a charming neighborhood called Brooklyn Heights. We were just off the Brooklyn Bridge and had some incredible neighbors, some of whom were famous and well known around the world.

Michael and I had two beautiful and wonderful daughters while we lived in Brooklyn Heights. I worked as a speech-language pathologist for the New York Board of Education. I loved my job, my co-workers and, most of all, the students. Our daughters had wonderful friends in our apartment complex and we lived quite near a very well known and excellent private school that Maya and Maura attended. Michael was teaching and taking post-graduate school level courses. He decided to pursue his doctorate degree and seemed to enjoy all of the challenges that went with it.

Then Michael was offered a job at Indiana University. We packed our belongings, children, and dog and moved to Bloomington, Indian, where Michael became a professor in the School of Music.

We bought a lovely house in a neighborhood that had children, teenagers, and many other middle class features. One neighbor teenage boy placed a rifle in his bedroom window that faced our house. I worked as a speech therapist in the public schools, some in rural communities. One of my student's father was an active member of the Ku Klux Klan. Knowing this student, working with her and the family was a real experience. And it was a warning for me to learn what to expect to experience. None of the students or their parents had ever been in a room with an African American person. I learned more about survival by living and working in Monroe County than I ever needed in New York City!

Marcia Hasler

I remember driving home to Farmersburg from Evansville when I was in med tech training at Deaconess Hospital in Evansville. Actually, I was a passenger, not the driver, along with a friend, Lana. Joanne Reeves was driving. We left Evansville at about 5 p.m. Joanne stopped and picked up a hitchhiker in a military uniform. He wanted a ride to Sullivan, Indiana. That was where my mom usually met me. Farmersburg is north of there. We dropped off the soldier. His aunt's house was down the street from "The Square" in Sullivan. I was let out on the square. My mom picked me up. Joanne and Lana went back down the highway to go home to Linton, Indiana. After I was home a few hours, or the next day, I got a call that they had had a wreck. A man crossed the center line and hit them head-on. Lana died instantly. Her neck was broken instantly. (She was a very tiny girl, barely five feet, and weighed ninety pounds or less.) Joanne was banged up, cuts and bruises and such, but nothing broken. It was over a fall weekend, maybe Thanksgiving. I went to the funeral in Linton. It was very sad. She was engaged to be married and one of two siblings.

Jackie Hayden

I remember in my sophomore year, I went to Mexico City with my best friend, who was an exchange student from there. When we landed, there were so many people at the airport that I asked Flavia if she knew of an important person on the plane. She said it was *me*. There was a parade of cars going to her home (a mansion) that night. It was so fun since I was a blond in Mexico, and all the boys were hanging around me. They had a huge party with a band on the winding staircase. I admired a bracelet on her mother's wrist and she took it off and gave it to me. Flavia had the dearest parents. They owned five hotels in Mexico City. She had four brothers. I liked Saturnino, but when I got home I kept corresponding with Jorge.

One day we went to their home in Acapulco. On the way down, their stupid dog bit me. I never did like Pomeranians! I remember skiing on the Pacific Ocean and going to La Quebrada and watching the divers dive from such high cliffs.

I was always treated like royalty—and only fifteen years of age!

Josephine Heady

One time...I was a secretary who signed up to be a part of the WAVES and they decided I should be trained as a metal smith. Out of 55 of us only 5 of us finished. I had the highest score. The man who had the same score as I did won a prize. But as a woman I didn't get anything.

I remember being stationed at the naval air station in Norfolk, Virginia. My job was to check the planes to make sure they were okay, not the engines, but as a metal smith. The planes were used to transport troops so we had to sit on the floor. The only seats were for the pilot and the co-pilot. We all had to wear parachutes. What I hated the most were the drills where we jumped from the plane. It was scary, but there wasn't anything I could do about it.

June Herman

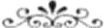

My memories of childhood revolve around a one-horse town called West Chicago, Illinois. It was a tiny village-type setting, 45 miles west of Chicago—thus its obvious name. It had one stoplight, one movie theatre, one bank, one dentist, as well as two grade schools and one high school.

My father was the proprietor of what was called "the general store." It was, indeed. Hard goods (appliances in the back), clothing for various ages of men and women in the front. My father and his cousin were head honchos. Since we (our family and theirs) were the only two Jewish families in town, it further stereotyped the idea that Jewish people were in business—of whatever kind. My family was quite successful in business—when you have a monopoly on the products, you have a leg up. The Christmas tree in the downtown square came from our front yard. Thus, we became the family known as what today we would call philanthropists because we were able.

Mine was a childhood that accepted us as the only Jewish family in town. There were vocal taunts toward me on occasion. What was said behind closed doors is beyond me. The taunts thrown at me made me aware of our religious differences but never made me back off my aggressive personality, one that remains to this day.

I had an older sister who was the image of what my father wanted for a daughter. She was attractive, tall, a talented piano player, and the polar opposite of me. I played baseball, she played "boys"— successfully till her death at 90 years.

My memories of my mother remain vivid. She was dominated by her husband, yet she was warm and reassuring during my formative years. She lived her final years in Florida—how I wish I could talk to her today.

I don't think I was ever very comfortable with my father. He showed much favoritism to my sister. No one used a "shrink" at that time (unfortunate). Perhaps I could have found much more about myself and my reactions.

At my venerable age (about to be double 8s) there is a lot to be said about my interactions with my family. And yet, I cope as best I can. Independence is of primary importance today. I never want to lose it!

Nancy Clark

"Where are you John Wesley?"

It happened here in Indianapolis, happened in the 1970s at the Indiana Convention Center. There was a worldwide convention of Methodist bishops and ministers. Here's the whole set up. Think about looking at 25,000 people. The convention hall was totally filled. Bishops from Africa in tribal costumes sat in the front of the stage. Wonderful! And there were others from all over the world in their magnificent costumes and colors.

Now the show: It was an original musical written by a local composer, geared to Methodists. "Where are you John Wesley when we need you now?" There was one set—a study of the minister. Portraits around on the wall were really real people sitting! The point was that each minister could not think about what to write about for their sermons.

My character was married to a minister, Mr. Milktoast. I was a suffragette in the 20's and I was the dominant wife. I remember when my door opened to the stage and I entered marching 4/4 holding my flag, all in black, a poke bonnet, singing my song. I depicted a strong personality and I am, period! I couldn't be anything else!

When I stopped the singing of the song, I addressed Reverend Milktoast. I knew he liked to take a nip. So, I was looking around and my eye settled on a big book on the library shelves on stage and inside the book was a 5th in the cut out pages. So I had righteous indignation! I was impassioned. (My character took over; I studied the Stanislavsky method.) I lost control and I took the book and hit him in the belly and that fella was not expecting that much momentum. He went flying across the room! When it happened, the audience believed it! It brought the house down.

I had a lot of good memories on stage, but that was the funniest. It stopped everything.

"Getting There"

Lee and I live here at Hooverwood. (He lives in the Alzheimer's unit. We've been married 60 years.) We had an airplane in the 60s and 70s. Statistics: Mooney Master, 4 place, single engine, capability of ten miles of gliding time. I loved that about the Mooney.

We were flying out from an airport in Florida to the Bahamas and we were heading for a quay—Little Abaco—so tiny that we had to set the plane down on a landing strip in Greater Abaco. We were about halfway out over the island of Bimini. Water was everywhere you could see. Our engine started sputtering. My husband said I turned white as a ghost.

I trusted my husband wholeheartedly. We have been in tight places in our lives before. He was not disturbed at all. He was cool. The engine stopped sputtering. It totally stopped, (We've got ten miles I thought and no place to go.) Then I am quiet. I am praying.

What he was doing under the fuselage of two big gas tanks? His instruments were telling him his gas tank was on empty and he had to convert to the other. But he didn't tell me that the engine might stop when he had to do this.

That was the scariest time of my life. Oh, Honey, did we have a wonderful time on that island! A most clear sky. A surge of falling stars on the beach. It was something to see. The harbor had a candy striped red and white light house. A lovely experience. Getting there was terrifying.

Joan Horwitz

I remember my wedding day, my honeymoon, and when my first child, a boy, was born.

The second time I was expecting, I wished for a girl, and that is what I had. My daughter graduated from Ohio State with a degree in education, and she has used it well. She also obtained her PhD from Ball State. After the graduation ceremony, we went to lunch with the family. My son-in-law gave an open house that evening. She has used her education well. She now has a very good job in education.

Anna Kafka

I remember when I was four years old, and I had the lead singing and acting role in the school play.

We lived in Lexington, Missouri. There were grape arbors in our yard, and we kept chickens. We had a German shepherd that we had to give away because he had bitten the postman. Our house did not have indoor plumbing; our bathroom was a small outhouse. There were hollyhocks in the gardens. I remember that the people who lived across the street from us were teachers. They owned a Victorian mansion. In their yard was a pond with water lilies in it and a bridge over it. Their yard reminded me of a Monet painting.

Eloise Kibler

I met my husband in the first grade. My husband served in the military on a destroyer in the Pacific, and I remember the day he returned home. I remember when we built our first house.

I experienced the thrill of being fortunate enough to adopt not one, but three children, each one so different from the other. The first was a beautiful baby girl; the second was a feisty, cute, blonde, blue-eyed boy; the third was a sweet but perpetually crying boy. Each child was totally different in personality. The girl was easy—she did everything correctly and well. The second was always a challenge—he had a temper, temper, temper! The third had a sweet, laid-back, artistic temperament. Looking back, I raised three children with totally different personalities!

When the third child arrived, the six-year-old and the four-year-old loved the baby and wanted to be helpful. Just after I brought the baby home, the four-year-old brought a whole quart of milk upstairs to feed the baby.

When the baby was six months old, a social worker came to check on us. The six-year-old, the eldest, wanted to show the social worker how smart the baby was to make sure we could keep him. The two older children lined up wooden blocks with letters on them. They also demonstrated, with a doll and buggy, how good they were with the baby. They were loving him up. We passed the inspection.

The youngest cried so much but the older children could entertain him and keep him happy. The older two would bicker with each other but not with Jimmy, the youngest. Jimmy just passed away at the age of 53. He was very artistic and he liked to write. The eldest two children live here, in Indianapolis.

Carol McElroy

I remember as a very little girl staying at my grandmother's home and taking off on a walk. I was probably around four years old, as my grandmother died when I was five. I didn't tell anyone. I just walked. I was not afraid, and I don't remember how far I walked. I must have returned back to my grandma's home because I'm here today! I remember her home and playing with some other children. I was very quiet and was surprised that I took off by myself.

I always knew right from wrong.

I played with other children in the fenced back yard. One girl wanted to go down to the cellar to the bathroom. She wanted to go "like a boy." This really upset me so I stayed away from her but probably did not tell my parents. This little girl did not seem very nice to me.

I was the firstborn of four children in my family. I remember my grandmother became ill and stayed upstairs a lot. She loved to cook and bake. She loved to raise flowers and had a birdbath in the fenced yard. Their house was connected to other houses on 2nd Street in Belleville, Illinois. It had a brick sidewalk around it.

I remember sitting in the living room on the floor by a large radio and everyone was very concerned and serious. The President was speaking about a war beginning. My daddy was not called to go fight, but my Aunt Dee became a WAC and my Uncle Norman was drafted into the army. Later he went to school on the GI bill and became a science teacher. He always had interesting stories to tell us, and he had a telescope. He also had a movie camera and made movies so it looked like magic.

My brother Roger (five years younger than me) and I were playing in the back yard of our house on Portland Avenue. Uncle Norman made a sparkly wand like a star. In the movie he waved it over me and I "disappeared." It was such fun! I still have the silent movie but the film is probably too brittle to watch. My son says I should have it put on a CD. Uncle Norman was my favorite uncle, and he never married. My Uncle Marshall went into the Army also and went to Germany. He married a German girl, and they had one daughter. He already had an adopted son and another son from another marriage. I have lost contact with him, but he was an artist and cartoonist. Uncle Norman died in 2000, but my husband and I visited him several times in Florida. He had banana, orange, and pineapple trees and a fishpond. He also had a wonderful record collection, which he left at our home in Belleville. I would sneak the records out and dance and sing to them. I wanted to be a dancer but never took lessons. My parents did not have the money, but I had two cousins in St. Louis who danced in recitals on the Admiral Boat on the Mississippi. I remember going on the boat with my cousins and dancing in the large ballroom. The decorations were beautiful and very elegant. I particularly loved the ladies' restrooms, different on each level. We explored the entire boat without our parents. What fun!

All my three uncles—Mom's brothers—and two sisters could play piano and any instruments by ear. There was also artistic talent on my mother's side. My grandpa was a draftsman at Scott Air Force Base. He painted pictures by numbers and did some painting on his own.

I am now oil painting and love it. I never knew I had any talent but always wanted to paint. About two years ago after my husband went "home to heaven," I started. I love it, and it is therapy for me. I'm using the right side of my brain, too. I want to write for my grandkids and have started a book. This is a good beginning for me. I want to write about my wonderful life with my husband, Tom, who was a doctor. He diagnosed himself with Multiple Sclerosis while studying neurology in his third year of medical school. We met when I was affiliated with IU School of Medicine in 1960.

When I was in high school, I wanted to be a secretary, but then changed my mind in the beginning of my junior year. I did not enjoy shorthand, and sitting at a desk all day seemed boring. I decided to switch to college prep and for a short time wanted to be a journalist. Then my mother planted an idea in my mind. She had been working as a nurse's aide at the local hospital and loved it. She said, "Why don't you become a nurse? You will always have a job."

The junior college was starting a nursing program so that way I could stay home and go to school. Then an opportunity arose for a scholarship with a loan from a nursing school in St. Louis, MO, across the river. I decided to pick what I thought was the best school, Deaconess Hospital across from the famous Forest Park Zoo. The idea was to have the nurses return to Belleville, IL. I wrote a letter and won the scholarship. At that time I had no plans, and it only cost $500 for three years of training. This was the first time I had been away from home, but I could come home on weekends. I started work at an insurance company during the summer to make extra money, but an article in the newspaper stated that I had won the scholarship and would be leaving in September. So that stopped my insurance job immediately.

I had been having pains in my side. My family doctor said it could be my appendix and that it would be best to have it removed before starting training. I had the surgery in August, which really prepared me for what to expect in training. I didn't count on the pain issue. My family doctor stated that I would probably marry a doctor and live happily ever after. That was not what I wanted, as I saw many doctor/nurse marriages end in divorce in my hometown. My family doctor had left his wife and married his nurse! I said in my heart, "I will *never* marry a doctor." Little did I know you should never say never.

Deaconess had an affiliation with the IU Medical School in Indianapolis at Riley Children's Hospital for four months during senior year. That sounded exciting to an 18-year-old who had always lived in Illinois and rarely traveled. I decided I wanted to be a nurse in a doctor's office instead of in a hospital. The class was divided into quarters, and you went to IU according to your last name. Since my name was Vetter, I was with the last group.

One of my best friends was in the group ahead of me, and we wrote letters often. She dated and was a party girl. She met a medical student named Tom who had a convertible and his dad was a surgeon in New Castle. They had horses. This impressed her but not me! Evidently she dated Tom who then "hid from her" during the last week she was there because he didn't want to get serious. Of course she was angry and told him not to even talk to me when I arrived.

I did meet him but was not interested at all because I wanted to date his sophomore roommate Jim. Tom was a freshman. His roommate would not ask me out, but Tom, wanting to make his roommate jealous, did ask me. We went out on a very snowy night with not many people on the road. We went to eat at the Hawthorne Room on N. Meridian Street. We had a good time but he asked me a weird question. "Do you believe in God?" I thought, "Of course I do, doesn't everyone?" I had always prayed to God as a young girl. Then he said, "I don't. I'm an atheist." "What kind of stupid person are you?" I thought.

We dated several more times but I wanted to date other students. He fixed me up with others and always asked me what I thought. They were nice but that was all. I guess he really liked me, but I didn't know this. Later in letters he had written but not sent, he said he wanted to marry me the first time we went out. What a surprise to me when I found the letter after he died.

He told me one time he loved me and I went into a panic. I awakened the next day with angioedema of the face, and my roommate asked what happened. I wouldn't go out as he kept calling and asking me why. I couldn't go to the student union looking like that. When he found out it was because my face was swollen, he thought it was funny.

One of the student nurses in my group was part American Indian and she was very mystical. She said she knew I would marry Tom because he had small hands. We dated, but I wasn't sure if he was the one. Then one day I missed breakfast and had to go to the snack bar. There was Tom ahead of me in line with another nurse. He had dated her earlier in the year. He said she had ironed his shirts, and I said I would not do his ironing.

But that was the turning point when I realized I was jealous and really cared for him. The rest of the story is we were pinned in February 1961, and I went back to St. Louis. We wrote every day and saw each other when we could. It was 250 miles each way. In one of the letters I wrote, "It was fate that we met." He wrote back, "There is no such thing as fate. I pursued you, and you had me running in circles."

I graduated in June, and Tom gave me an engagement ring instead of a "yellow polka dot bikini." I moved to Indianapolis in August 1961, and we were married November 24, the day after Thanksgiving. He had that weekend off.

It has been a wonderful journey and I am so blessed to have two precious children, a boy and a girl, and four grandchildren. I also worked in Tom's office as his nurse. Tom was majoring in chemistry and changed his mind the last year at Wabash. It is amazing how God put us together.

Sue Meyer

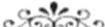

I was living in Laredo, Texas, as the wife of an instructor fighter pilot. After Christmas we decided to take a short trip to Monterey, Mexico. It was a cold day when we started out. We boarded the train, heading south toward Mexico. The afternoon was spent in the train's club car, as the regular seats were uncomfortable. The train pulled into Monterey and we headed for town for sightseeing and a Mexican dinner along with a *cerioca* or two.

In Monterey, there was a muddy mountain with rocks to traverse. Our destination was a beautiful waterfall. We took a donkey ride down the mountain led by a guide. Six month's pregnant, I felt like the Virgin Mary.

It was cold outside and I was wearing a black and white checked coat which had a black velvet collar. My flat shoes made walking difficult. The donkey was tame and I began to feel comfortable that he would to lead me down carefully and away from the slippery edges. The two people I was with smiled at the scene of a fashionable, pregnant woman on a donkey.

Evvy Moss

My First Meeting with Cousin Vivi

The year was 1967. I was a single, 24-year-old Hoosier and second cousin to Vivi Boas when we first met. I was hitchhiking through Europe in a search for my family roots. (Vivi's mother and my father were first cousins, both born in Germany. In their 50s, Liselotte and Ernest Boaz, at the time, and their daughter, Vivi, immigrated from San Paulo to Pully, Switzerland.)

The Boas family made their home in Pully. When I was 25 years old in 1967, I was invited to a family dinner upon my arrival in the city of Pully on my familial search. As it turned out, Vivi, being a bit of a rebellious 16-year-old, arrived late.

Vivi's presence, upon arriving home and entering the formal living room, made a statement. The petite, beautiful, brown-eyed girl with thick, black hair, of sallow skin and swarthy complexion and with the body type of a Degas ballet statue, won my heart at our first meeting. With a soft and gentle voice, she spoke impeccable English with somewhat of a British accent. Of course, her parents, who were of European *puntlick* and background, were most annoyed with their late daughter. And they let it be known that they were not happy!

Vivi and I had a little time together, but she won my heart! And, at that very moment I felt that I would always be her loving second cousin, friend, and protector—and, I was, up until her dying day in November of 2011, when my sons and I were by her side.

Vivi and I shared much from that 1967 meeting to 2011 and much happened in both of our lives. Vivi married her high school boyfriend in San Paulo. Two children arrived. Soon after the arrival of her second son, about 1978, Vivi sought a divorce and moved from Mexico to Dana Point, California. There, she enrolled in a prestigious fine arts program. She was a gifted artist and sculptor and her world was viewed through the lens of an artist. She already had a couple of paintings in the Louvre.

In the meantime, I married and had three children. Vivi's parents came to visit us in Indianapolis, and our parents vacationed together in Arizona.

Through all the years, Vivi made frequent trips between Indianapolis and Dana Point, and I, in turn, travelled to California to be with Vivi and her sons. We shared Jewish holiday observances—she was present at happy, special occasions, as well as the sad ones, too. We traveled together extensively through Europe. Vivi was always the interpreter as she was fluent in five languages. A very special time was when Vivi was with the Moss Family on a special one-week trip to Israel in 1996.

Once my cousin and I were on the way to Braunschweig cemetery in Germany. Her father had died. We planned on visiting his grave. We arrived at the Braunschweig train depot and hailed a taxi. We directed the driver to the Jewish cemetery. We arrived around 4 p.m. on a Friday. It was locked.

The cab driver suggested going to City Hall. We went there. They couldn't help. No key was available. The cab driver returned us to the cemetery. We spent an hour surveying the area, trying to figure out how to get over the spiked fence. We made a plan. The cab driver and I would form a bridge with our hands. Vivi was booted up and over the spiked fence. She searched and searched for the grave. She found it. She was crying. I was crying on the outside. She left a rock on the stone. Now to get Vivi out of the cemetery! She climbed over with the cab driver catching her. He drove us back to the train depot.

We stayed connected by phone or by being together face-to-face. Some times were more special and memorable than others. We experienced the good and not-so-good sharing and always in spite of the cross country miles that separated us.

And then it happened that Vivi's behavior became almost nonsensical at times. Her son shared that her day-to-day behavior was becoming almost problematic. At the urging of an elder brother and me, a medical consultation occurred—Mad Cow Disease was the initial finding. This disease had hardly ever been found in the US, but there were a few documented cases on record. What would happen next?

The decision was made for Vivi to move from California to Syracuse, New York to be with her eldest son and his family. Once she moved, another medical consultation was done and a very different diagnosis was made. Vivi was facing a very aggressive and early on-set Alzheimer's disease. The prognosis was premature death, and a very slow and ugly one at that.

Vivi remained in Syracuse and was placed in a nursing home facility. On one of my early visits to see her and unbeknownst to anyone, we went to a local cinema to see Michael Jackson's *This is It*. Before the film, I arranged for Vivi to have a manicure for her beautiful, long fingers and nails, which had been neglected. Naughty we were, but we had such a good time!

Needless to say, over time, Vivi only deteriorated. Everything about her changed, but she always knew who I was until one of my last visits. By then, Vivi had been transferred to a homecare facility in Topeka, Kansas, as her son and his family had moved for business reasons. Upon my arrival at the facility, Vivi was rolled out in a wheelchair by an attendant. I was in shock! She appeared almost "witch-like." She was skin and bones, face ever so gaunt, her high-boned cheeks were sunk in, her hair was in disarray, and she had no recollection of me, her loving cousin, Evvy. My drive home from Kansas to Indiana was a very sad one. The reality of losing my beloved cousin, Vivi, had become a reality.

Reality did set in when I received a call from her son, Rene. Mother was on her death bed and would I come? Of course. I went to Kansas. And, for four days, there was a slow and agonizing bedside vigil. She deserved better, as does anyone.

I mourned but was left with the plaguing question— did Vivi ever come to accept that she had been adopted? When I first met her in 1967, her parents shared this information with me in private while showing me a film of Vivi's years growing up. Vivi, as the story went, was born of one of Liselotte and Ernest's household servants. Ernest and Liselotte, who were around fifty years of age at the time and childless, decided to make Vivi their own child. No one ever knew if there was a formal adoption or not.

Vivi had never been told she was adopted! In later years of our relationship, she indicated to me that at times she had wondered. What prompted her to wonder? Her parents were obviously of western European lineage and Vivi, with her sallow skin, beautiful coal black hair, and somewhat almond dark brown eyes, bore no physical resemblance to either parent. Vivi concluded that she knew of familial instances where offspring and parents were quite different in physical makeup and for sure there was no adoption. So, she would end up reassuring herself that she was the biological daughter of Liselotte and Ernest. Although I knew otherwise, I did not have the heart to share with her what her mother, Liselotte, had shared with me all those years ago. That is my secret! Also, my secret is how much I miss, how much I had loved Vivi!

Sheila Nachlis
as told to Bonnie Maurer

"Three life-changing events"

1.
1972, Hurricane Agnes. We were living in Pennsylvania. After days of rain, the Susquehanna was reaching its limit. When we were awakened by a neighbor, we had to evacuate. I had a son 1 month old and one 7. Of course, we didn't know what to take. We took all the wrong things—everything for the 1 month old and nothing for ourselves—no clothes, no mementos. We went to my in-laws out of the flood plain. And after a week, we were allowed back. We had trouble getting back in. The dykes had broken and the whole valley was inundated. Furniture was thrown against the wall. Nothing was salvageable in the house. Our whole life was piled at the curb to be taken to the dump by a "Shovel truck." And that was devastating—not knowing how to get our life back together again.

In the event of a disaster, one should take pictures. I lost my wedding album. We found two crystal glasses floating up and saved them on the table and then when my neighbor came to help, he knocked the table and the crystal glasses shattered. I salvaged every single piece of silverware I found in the mud. Nobody had flood insurance. We found our car in someone else's yard. The government put us up in another city and we eventually built a new house— on the top of a hill.

2.

1976. I woke up one morning feeling ill and weak. I couldn't pick up the teapot and by the end of the day I was paralyzed. Doctors were not able to diagnose me, but it was spinal related. I was sent to rehab 25 miles away from home, where I stayed for nine months. Learning to walk again was grueling. I had surgeries. I was a piano teacher and taught privately. I had two hand surgeries and gained functionality. Over the years, things got weaker. I went from a cane to a walker to a scooter and that was the reason I had to move to Hooverwood.

3.

My Mom had died and my husband died. I was living in a senior independent community. I was divinely happy there. They called it a villa. My condition deteriorated. My kids worried about me, so I moved to Hooverwood. I found my niche here and I love the bonding with my grandkids, the hugging and the touching as my daughter-in-law drives by everyday. So, I came in on a gurney on a long trip form Pennsylvania. Quite honestly I was not a happy camper when I arrived. I had to get on anti-depression pills. A terrible thing to think this is going to be your last move. But I've discounted those thoughts in favor of being close to family and watching my grandchildren grow up. And even my son from New York comes in to see me.

Alex Star

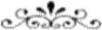

I was born in Szil, Hungary, in 1926. When I was twelve years old, my father died. I went to the city of Gyor to be with my brother, Lali. My mother and sister remained at home. I stayed in Gyor for six years.

In 1944, one thousand American bombers flew over Gyor and bombed it. When I saw the bombers, I was wearing my armband with the star. The sound in Gyor as the bombs hit the factories and train tracks was impossibly hushed, quiet, even holy as compared to the impossibly deafening crash as an American bomber came down. Its parts mixed with broken, yet to be assembled, *Messerschmidt* aircraft. That sound was all-consuming, as was the cold. The Hungarians managed to shoot down a couple of planes. I remember the smoke plumes were higher than my grandfather's firewood stacks. My brother, Lali, took care of me in Gyor, and I hid with him in a haystack and in a barn in the countryside of Hungary.

After the bombing of Gyor, I went home. My mother, sister, and I were deported to a ghetto. And on my way to the ghetto for the first time, I saw the Hungarian Nazis riding bicycles and motorcycles and waving axes and knives. They took no prisoners.

In the ghetto, all of the young people had to work on a farm. On the day they first sent me into the fields to work, my mother and sister were packed up and shipped to Auschwitz.

I remember the last time I saw my mother and my baby sister.

I was in several different work camps. One day I was moved to a new camp with about one hundred and fifty other people. Of those one hundred and fifty, I am the only one left alive. Eventually, I escaped the camp and went back to Szil as the Russians closed in on Budapest. When I arrived in Szil, I found the Hungarian Nazis had commandeered my house and converted it into a storehouse.

I was sneaking around town barefoot, having cut off my wooden shoes because my feet were so swollen and cold from the winter. It was almost Christmas.

After hiding several days in Szil, a friend told me to leave as he was in fear for my life. I jumped a train in Moson-Magyar. Hungarian Nazis caught me. Luckily, in a military court run by the Germans, a Hungarian colonel recognized me. He told me to tell the Germans I was running from the Russians. I did that and was set free.

Then I went to the city of Szombathely. When I arrived I was so desperate for a job. By this time I was 19 years old and I still had no papers. A friend gave me documents. I was an electrician by trade, but official papers meant nothing. I still had my name, and it betrayed me. I had to run again after I met a man, who after looking at my papers had dialed the phone. He shielded his eyes but I saw them darting in my direction.

In Austria, I was digging ditches again. I weighed 95 pounds. My bones poked into my skin and stretched my nerves. I was rickety and weak. We kept hearing that the Russians would save us and they came. They left three hundred of us in a barn. We were the ones who could hardly stand. They shipped the others to Siberia.

The Nazis left. I crawled back to Szil. I knew a Hungarian police chief there. He got me a horse and buggy so I could go house to house and collect clothes to wear. My brother returned and he got me a maintenance job. My other brother came back from Siberia in 1946, pieces of shrapnel still stuck in his calf. Two hundred pieces of metal in that leg, one for each member of my family lost.

In 1947, I left Hungary for the last time. I traveled to France.

In France, I bumped into a comrade from the camps. I went to work in a salt mine. I operated the cable car, which went sixty miles underground. In France, I worked for three years until I received a passport and departed for the United States.

When I reached the United States, my uncle picked me up from Ellis Island and made me throw all my clothes away.

Of my family, only three brothers and a sister survived.

I would like to visit my father's grave. I don't know where the others are buried.

Janet Stillerman

I remember going downtown shopping with my mother in the 1940s. We lived at the corner of College and Watson Road. The streetcar stopped in front of our house. There weren't suburban shopping centers, so if you wanted to go shopping you went downtown. There was Ayres, Blocks, Wassons, and Strauss, and we walked from one store to the other. Mother also had a few favorite smaller stores, like Charles Meyers Co. After shopping for a while, Mother would take me to my favorite restaurant, the L.S. Ayres Tearoom, for lunch. For dessert, I would order the ice cream princess. Her head and shoulders were made of china and her dress was ice cream, beautifully decorated. When we were ready to leave, all the children could pick a toy prize to take home. The boys' gifts were wrapped with blue ribbon and the girls' with pink. Everyone got dressed up to go to the tearoom, with hats and gloves. It was fun to get dressed up with a pretty dress.

After I married and had children, I would take them downtown shopping and we would go to the Ayres Tea Room for lunch. The children's lunches were now served in a big bandanna, which they could take home, but they still had the toy chest with the boys' and girls' gifts wrapped up in it.

Larry Teich

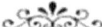

"Al the Tie"

Hey! Where do you want me to start? How about the beginning? I must have been eight or nine when I met the "Dutchman," Dutch Shultz. My father, Abraham, (who would later be known as "Al the Tie)—you will read about that a little later) was a cab driver in New York City. He took me to a coffee shop at 125th Street and Lexington Avenue, where Dutch offered Dad a job, and in that instant he became a member of the Jewish Mafia. Things were great! We got a new Oldsmobile and I had a charge account at Max Moscowitz, a clothing store on Bleecker Street, where the Jewish Mafia shopped. I even met Benjamin Segal, aka "Bugsy;" however, I learned very early *never* to call him that.

I was born in the Bronx in 1925, but we moved to Manhattan and lived in the Oliver Cromwell Hotel which is located at Central Park West. To coin a phrase, I was "living large." When I was fifteen, a tailor came to our house to custom-fit my dad for a suit. I entered the room and the tailor greeted me by name. Dad asked him how he knew me and he told him that he made all of my suits. Needless to say, being in the Jewish Mafia benefited the entire family.

Like most JM families, we spent a portion of our summers in the Catskill Mountains. One afternoon I was playing softball at the Plaza Hotel in South Fallsburg, NY. I was rounding third base when the third baseman shoved his glove right in my face. We were immediately separated by his bodyguard. It turns out that this kid's father was Louis "Lepke" Buchalter, one of the key members of "Murder Incorportated," and he was in the hotel, meeting with my dad. While the men were undoubtedly discussing less than legal affairs, their sons were not going to get into a fist fight!

One night in 1940, when I was about 15, we went to Madison Square Garden to see a hockey game between New York and Toronto. After the game, we went across the street to eat at Frank's Steakhouse. I sat down while my dad went to talk to someone. When he returned, he pinned an envelope to the inside of my coat. After dinner I went home alone. My dad came in a little later and retrieved his envelope. In it were thirteen one thousand dollar bills. As it turns out, the game was fixed!

It was a great time to be living well in Manhattan. We would go to Ette Italian Steakhouse at 125th Street, in Harlem. It was just down the street from the famous Apollo Theater, where we met Duke Ellington, Cab Calloway, and Hazel Scott, a jazz pianist, who would marry U.S. Congressman, Adam Clayton Powell, Jr. Dad was active in the Harlem community and was instrumental in fundraising efforts there.

So how did my dad become "Al the Tie?" Well, Dad was also involved in many legitimate business concerns. He financed a number of businesses and, unlike Al Capone, he always paid his taxes so he was never in trouble with the IRS. One of these businesses was being a dress manufacturer. Dad would take the excess silk fabric and have it made into beautiful neckties. When someone would compliment him, he would take off his tie and give it to that person. Damon Runyon, the famous New York columnist, heard about this and gave him the moniker, "Al the Tie." Of course, to me he was just Dad.

Jim Trulock

We misspell and mispronounce names all over the country. Hey, it's America. To us, it is Versales and Cayro and New Maadrid. Anyway, the story's not about that or the town we were in—Phoenix City, Alabama. It's about feeling dumb when I was expected to act smart. I was fifteen, in a hotel room with a bunch of con men trying as best I could to be one of them. I didn't know how, so I just tried to look cool and know what was going on even if I didn't.

Phoenix City was a mobbed out, wide-open town just across the Chattahoochee River from Fort Benning, Georgia. It had open gambling, all night clip joints, strip clubs, and whore houses. Something for the boys. Anything, actually. General George Patton had once threatened to bulldoze it down with his tanks, a notion that was, I'm sure, profoundly unpopular with his troops. I knew about these things in an abstract way. I'd never smoked a cigarette, had a drink, and sure hadn't been in one of those houses. I was just beginning to understand my fascination with girls and being wild but not really engaged in anything beyond kissing Beverly Barker in the Garfield Theater in Indianapolis.

We were in a large corner hotel suite on the third floor. The black bellhop had brought drinks and sandwiches and a big peach pie. It was summer and still hot. Maybe it was the sponge shirt. I was the only kid and it seemed to me the only one not wearing a straw hat.

They all had phony names. There was Big Al Hamilton and Little Al Smith, Bob Trout, Ernie High from New York, Harry Chalmers, S. Clyde Williams, John R. Winfrey (my father), and me. I was still called Jimmy. They were all there to cut up the South.

Let me explain. There was a sweet con working in the South first employed by S. Clyde whereby an employer paid a go between big dollars to keep the union out, not that anyone in that room had anything to do with a union. It could be very complex but it was a gold mine with countless shafts. It was based on bigotry, fear, and that universal accouterment of the rich: greed. Enter the con man. Pay me and we won't organize your negroes. They used another word. What a deal, what a load off their backs, what benevolent care of their people to help them not be forced into a union. "The Lord works in mysterious ways his wonders to perform."

They were all there to divide up the territory. We had been working central Florida and the mining and manufacturing that went on there. Medium sized businesses run by self-made men. They were the best marks there were. They couldn't make mistakes. They were minor gods on their own minor turf just trying to keep on top of their own minor world. John R. Winfrey could help.

But now it had become so sweet that the grifters in the room had to not step on each other's deals. So after a long and sweaty afternoon of eating pie and listening to bullshit, the turf splitting began.

Dad got Tennessee. The real plums, though, were the Deep South states of Mississippi, Alabama, and Georgia. The unions of the CIO (Congress of Industrial Organizations) were feared and despised by Southern business owners. They were thought of as a combination of Yankees, Communists, and the Devil incarnate. Their way of life was being challenged just like in the Civil War or, as they called it, The War Between the States. Why, if workers organized into unions—who knows, they might even want to vote. These race-mixing Yankee unions must be kept out at all costs. Here's the scam: these con artists picked businesses that the unions weren't interested in anyway. All the cons put on phony Southern accents so as to seem like one of them. For some, though, it was impossible. Hell, as far as I know, Ernie had never been West of the Catskills.

Here's how I remember these guys. I'll start with Ernie High. He was about 5'4" both ways. He had a neck bigger than my head, bigger than his, too, and always wore tailor-made clothes. He had on a silk suit. He had a little pencil-thin mustache and wore the biggest star sapphire pinky ring I have ever seen. He would always ask how I was doing, and if he knew I was going to be there, he would always bring a book for me. He later went to prison.

Dad had worked with Harry Chalmers and S. Clyde Williams in Louisiana where Dad had made his biggest score a few years before. It was the McAllhaney Brothers. They made Tabasco sauce on Avery Island, Louisiana. It was over ten grand, and they were rich for a while. Anyway, Harry always had some new gorgeous young woman on his arm every time we saw him. He had on a wide-brim straw hat, a brown Hawaiian shirt with big red flowers on it, and was the only guy I had ever seen in sandals. He had a pronounced Chicago accent—you know, Da Bears—and was somehow always made uncomfortable by my presence. At least that is how it seemed to me. Perhaps it was because his girlfriends thought I was cute. I was fifteen—they were cute, too.

Bob Trout was tall, thin, wore horn-rimmed glasses, a grey suit, and looked all business. It was deceiving. He had a way about him that would make you insist on buying your share of the Brooklyn Bridge. He got Georgia.

Big Al and Little Al were a pair. They worked in tandem. Big Al had a kind of soft demeanor and a gentleness to him. He must have been 6'3" and always deferred to Little Al. It was the early 1950s, and even these wise guys couldn't figure them out. It was twenty years later before I did. Of course, they were gay and a couple. They pulled the con together and were very good at it. They got Alabama and now the story turns tragic.

Big Al was deathly afraid of the cops. He would take great pains to avoid uniformed officers. I don't know the whole story, but I believe it had something to do with his experience related to his sexual orientation. He came walking out of a hotel in Birmingham in 1954, and a policeman was standing there. Al started running, the officer in hot pursuit. He ordered him to halt and when he didn't, he shot and killed Al Hamilton.

Little Al Smith was from the Bronx and a foot shorter than Big Al and until the untimely death of his partner always, so it seemed, used the imperial "we." I know this seems contradictory, but he looked like a cross between a Hasidic rabbi and a Chihuahua. He wore fine clothes, and that day had on a beautiful blue silk tee shirt and a bright blue headband on his Panama. He smoked great big cigars, which, when he could get there on time, Big Al lit. I told him I thought his shirt was neat; he calmly got up, went in the next room, came out in a minute with another one on, and threw the blue silk at me. "Keep it, Jimmy. It's yours." No matter how uncomfortable I felt in the room with these dandies, I came out a winner.

And now for Stan Williams, or S. Clyde, as he was called. There was a brilliance about him the likes of which I had and have never seen. He was wearing a white linen suit with a lavender handkerchief exploding from his pocket. It was as if a spotlight beamed down on him. I had first met him in New Orleans in a tavern on Canal Street where shysters and cons hung out. That was back in 1946. He had once given me $5 to sing the second verse of the "Star Spangled Banner," which I did. Few people know it so I was the phenomenon that day. Hey, I also knew the third verse, but he didn't ask about that. He could see, though, that Glenn (my father's real name) was training his kid in the art of the sweet talk trade.

S. Clyde was a legend among the people in the room. He, so the story goes, pulled this con on the Kingfish, Huey P. Long, for big time money. He was the prince of Flim Flam at least for now. While we

73

were eating the sandwiches I said, "I'll bet you a dollar I can say a word backwards quicker than you can." He replied, "You're on." I had worked this out just to get his money. The word was Constantinople. I had heard this done on the radio by a comedian named Professor Backwords.

"We'll start on the count of three. Okay?"

"Okay."

"One, two, three, Elponitnatsnoc," he said before I could get out the first syllable. He smiled condescendingly and said "I'll give it back if you sing that second verse again."

I looked around the room and they were all laughing at me. No way, I was older and wiser now. I sure wasn't going to humiliate myself even more in front of all these guys.

"No. You keep it Stan," I said. He glared at me. He didn't say it but I knew what that look meant. It meant never call me that in public. And I never did again.

As happens so often with con men, he was on top of the world one day, in desperate trouble the next. A few years later in Florida I got up one morning and there he was bedraggled, stuporous, unkempt, and hung-over, sleeping on our couch. He had been rolled and was broke. He had on a suit that should have been thrown away. S. Clyde was Stan again and he was silent and in a world of his own. Dad gently got him up and took him somewhere unknown to me. I'm sure he gave him money, but it was the last I ever saw of him. Some years later he was killed when his car was hit by a train at a crossing in Louisiana. The circumstances I will never know. I always thought it could have been murder.

The meeting began to break up as it was getting dusk. Trout left early. Had some business, he said. S. Clyde was getting hungry and had a reservation at some supper club. He took Harry with him. The suite belonged to the Als, and Ernie's wife was picking him up in front of the hotel. He couldn't drive. You didn't learn that kind of thing on the lower East side where he grew up.

Dad and I said goodbye to Big Al and Little Al. I thanked Little Al for the shirt again. He took the big stogie out of his mouth and gave me a kind of Talmudic nod and Dad and I went down the hall to the elevator. Before we got on he said, "You know what you did wrong, don't you?"

"Yeah," I said. "I called Stan *Stan*."

"We are friends but he wants to be called S. Clyde in front of others. You knew that didn't you?"

"Yes, I was mad at him for winning my dollar."

"Stan has a way of doing that. That's why he's S. Clyde." He put his arm around me, patted me on the shoulder and we got on the elevator, left the building and went back to our motel.

Mom and Dave had been swimming in the pool, and we were all tired. We ate supper at the restaurant across the highway, went back to the room, and went to bed. The next day, we kind of slept in and didn't leave until about ten o'clock. Nashville, here we come. It started out hot and got sizzling hot, so we drove up the road in our '49 three-holer Buick with all the windows down. Cars didn't have air conditioners then.

The waves of heat bounced off the blacktop pavement and when you looked out the back window of the Buick, the cars following us a quarter of a mile or so behind seemed to be traveling ten feet off the ground. When we passed a field with cows, they were dancing in place in the air. That's hot.

Dave and I were starting to make noises that boys make. Dave had made this wonderful discovery whereby if you put your hand in your opposite armpit, cup it just right and come down with your arm you can make a wondrous sound guaranteed to offend. I could never do this so had to revert to the tried and true method of what is called "raspberries." Dad was getting tired of this and was only moments away from uttering the dreaded and fearsome oath. "That's it. I'm going to stop this car and then you're both in trouble."

Mom interceded in a calm and even-tempered way. "You boys quiet down," she said and placidly said to Dad, "Glenn, I'll need to stop in the next town." He would always comply. She could mediate tension really well. Dave and I kept quiet and began looking at road signs. Gadsden: 4 miles. Okay.

We went on down the road and around a sweeping curve, through a woods and there it was, a big sign put up by the Chamber of Commerce welcoming one and all (providing you were white) to Gadsden.

Most small towns in the South in those days had two types of places that were air- conditioned: the drug stores and the movie houses. We traveled down the main drag to the town square and there it was: a banner emblazoned across the front window of Hogan's Cut-Rate Drugs announcing "Cooled by Carrier." We pulled in a diagonal parking spot three doors down from the cool paradise. Mom said, "I'll be right back," and Dad said, "Okay, we'll just wait." What?

Dave and I just sat there dumbfounded. Five minutes seemed like the preview of hell hour. Dad started getting antsy, and we sure did, too. Dave started to do his trick, and the sweat in his armpit made the potential really great, close to record-breaking, but before that could actually take place Dad said, "Boys." That's all it took, we were out of that Buick in no time flat, heading toward Hogan's.

Dave got to the door first, Dad and I right behind. What we witnessed then, I will always remember. There was Mom, pretty as a picture in her red and white sundress sitting at the soda fountain counter facing away from it, toward us, smiling. And behind her were four, tall cherry phosphates lined up just waiting for us. She knew her man. She knew her family.

So we males sauntered up to the swivel stools, Dad kissed Mom, and we turned toward the counter like in a Busby Berkley movie, put the straws in our mouths and enjoyed the best cherry phosphates ever

77

slurped. We stayed a while soaking up the cool, nosed through the notions, bought a *True Romance* magazine, a *Crime Reporter*, a "Plastic Man" comic book and a Daffy Duck, got back in the car and drove on down the sticky road. We made Nashville that night, content that we were the beloved sheep of the gentle shepherdess and that whatever happened next would be faced together.

Agnes V. Vogel

I remember cooking my first meal for my father. My mother was sick and I was the oldest child. I had to cook dinner.

I remember trying to ride a bicycle.

I remember the first time I met my husband.

I remember when my sister broke my china doll.

I remember staying in Paris before coming to America. It was a wonderful time. My father rode on the train to the border, and he found a Hungarian woman on the train who looked out for me while traveling to Paris. I stayed at a beautiful hotel. It was the best time of my life. I was there for three months and spent my time seeing the sights. I spent a lot of time visiting museums. There were Holocaust survivors there from all over Europe and we spent time together.

Bronka Zabelin

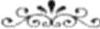

I remember the day when I was ten years old, and my sister made me an aunt!

I was living with my sister, who was twelve years older than I was. On the evening of April 1st, she went into labor and arrangements were made for me to go to her friend's house. It was not too long ago that I had just come to be with my sister and her husband, so she was learning about the responsibilities of caring for a child.

Arlene, my sister, left after dinner and the nice lady and I shared a banana. It was difficult staying with someone I didn't really know. When I woke up that morning, the lady told me that I had a niece born at 6:45 a.m. on April 2, 1965. Her name was Wendi Dawn Letbery. She weighed 7 pounds and was 19 inches long.

I was so proud, I went to school and at recess I told everyone about it. I made a song about the information and created the first "rap" song.

I was told about how my sister was twelve years old when I was born and how she adored me and did everything for me and always bought me things. I was determined to do the same for Wendi Dawn. Every time I got some money, I put it in her little bank.

Wendi lost her mittens with the strings on them the winter before she was one year old. I went to the department store on Devon Avenue, and I bought her a pink pair of mittens for a dollar. I told the lady I was buying them for my niece's birthday on April 2nd. She wrapped them up and I told her I would wait until her birthday to give them to her.

My sister, of course, talked me into letting her open the gift.

What was I thinking! The young eleven-year-old girl who adored her niece did not think that in April Wendi wouldn't need those mittens!

That summer we went to our summer cottage. Arlene talked me into letting us take the money from Wendi's bank to go on the vacation. Of course, that money was from a lot of people, but I was in charge of the bank. Yes, we had a great time spending Wendi's money, yes we did.

Dancer Biographies

Stuart Coleman began training in 2005 under the tutelage of Keith Lee in Lynchburg, Virginia. In 2007, he joined Virginia School of the Arts where he trained and performed until he graduated in 2010. Upon graduating from VSA, he enrolled in Butler University under the instruction of Michelle Jarvis, Marek Cholewa, Susan McGuire, and others. Stuart has attended numerous summer intensives throughout his training: Alonzo King's LINES Ballet, Alvin Ailey American Dance Theatre, Paul Taylor Dance Company, and Ballet West. His choreography has been featured in concerts produced by Butler Ballet, Virginia School of the Arts, and Dance Theatre of Lynchburg. This is Stuart's first season as an apprentice.

Emily Dyson received her BFA in Ballet Pedagogy from the University of Oklahoma, where she performed with Oklahoma Festival Ballet and Contemporary Dance Oklahoma. She began ballet training in Houston, TX with Gilbert Rome and Victoria Vittum and was later inspired by Austin Hartel to study modern. She trained with 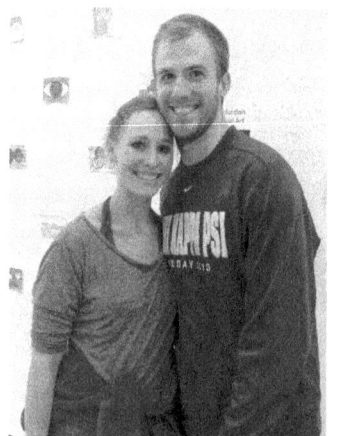 Paul Taylor Dance Company, American Ballet Theatre, The Joffrey, Washington School of Ballet, and Atlanta Ballet. Emily enjoys teaching around the city and passing forward her love of dance to younger students. This is her 4th DK season.

Brandon Comer began his dance training at The Dance Refinery in Indianapolis and graduated from Center Grove High School in Greenwood, IN, where he was very active in the musical and theatre department. He competed in ESPN's National Hip Hop Competition, performed at local theaters, and was a part of The Young Tanzsommer Arts Festival, which included a tour of Austria, Germany and Italy. This is Brandon's 6th season with DK.

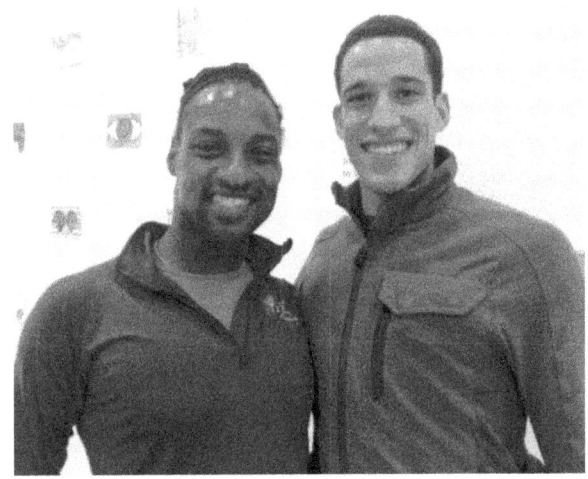

Justin Sears-Watson began dancing while majoring in vocal performance at the University of Evansville, and joined a ballet class for fun! He trained with Anna Reznik, and Alexei Kremnev of Chicago's Joffrey Academy, Cincinnati Ballet, and Giordano Jazz Dance Chicago's scholarship program. He danced with Giordano Jazz Dance Chicago II, Thodos Dance Chicago, and Inaside Dance Chicago. Justin currently teaches Ballet, Modern, Jazz, and Hip Hop, and choreographs for competition at Indy Dance Academy. This is Justin's 4th DK season.

Phillip Crawshaw is an Indianapolis native and a graduate of Anderson University with a Bachelor of Arts in Family Science and Psychology with a minor in Dance Performance. While at Anderson University he began his training in dance as well as participated in numerous dance, musical theatre, opera and choral performances. He danced with Gregory Hancock Dance Theatre in Carmel, before joining DK. This is Phillip's 2nd DK season as an apprentice.

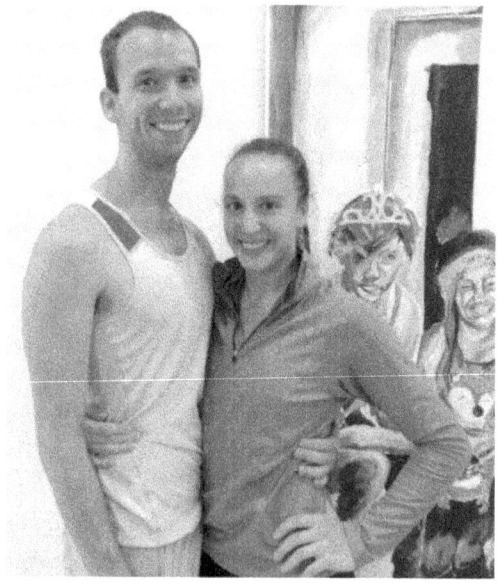

Aleksa Lukasiewicz originally from Novi, Michigan began her serious dance training at Geiger Classical Ballet Academy. She continued her studies at Butler University where she graduated in 2011 with honors and a BFA in Dance Performance. Aleksa's training also includes summer intensives such as Hubbard Street and a two month study abroad trip to Lithuania. This is Aleksa's 4th season with DK.

Jillian Godwin began her dance training in Indianapolis at Dance Magic Performing Arts Center and graduated from Broad Ripple High School, Center for the Performing and Visual Arts. She has also trained at Chautauqua Institution School of Dance and American Ballet Theatre's Summer Intensive. Jillian attended River North Chicago Dance Company's summer intensive in 2010 and 2012, where she was accepted on scholarship. Most recently, she was named one of Indy's top ten most intriguing artists in 2012. This is Jillian's 12th DK season.

Zach Young trained at Columbia Performing Arts Centre in Columbia, Missouri, where he studied under Karen Mareck Grundy, Lisa Geger, Sean

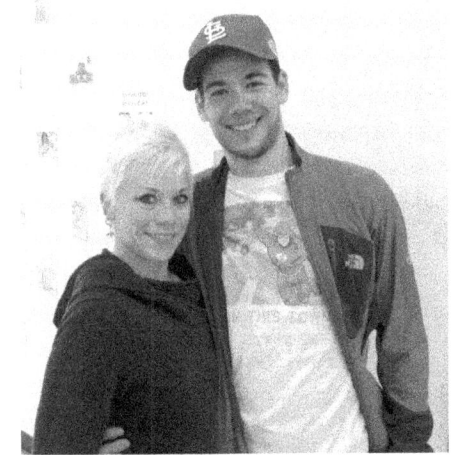

France and Jen Lee. He participated in summer intensives and workshops with River North Dance Chicago, Mark Morris, L.J. Ballard, Gary Hubler and Dante Adela. He has worked with contemporary choreographers Benoit Swan Pouffer, Jamar Roberts and Angel Fraser-Logan, and as a guest artist with the Cuban National Ballet. Zach also is trained in Tae Kwon Do and holds a first-degree black belt. Previously, he danced for the Cedar Lake Youth Ensemble, Cedar Lake II and the Missouri Contemporary Ballet. This is Zach's 7th season with DK.

Mariel Greenlee, originally from Vestal, NY, received her BA in Dance from Point Park University. She studied in New York City at The Martha Graham Center for Dance, Dance Space (DNA), STEPs, the Paul Taylor School, the Joffrey Ballet School and the David Parsons Workshop. Mariel received the Individual Artist grant from the IAC in 2007, 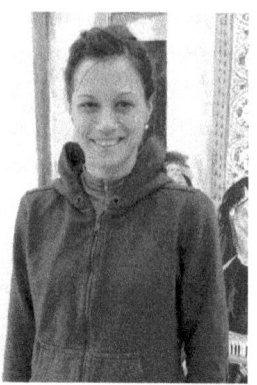 and she was a 2010 creative renewal fellow with the Indiana Arts Council. Mariel also teaches ballet and modern dance locally. This is Mariel's 10th DK season.

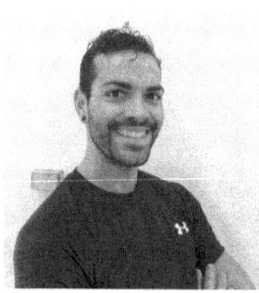 **Timothy June** is originally from Enfield, CT. His dance training began at New England Dance Conservatory. Timothy continued studies at Miami City Ballet, Boston Ballet, the Rimsky-Korsakov Conservatory in St. Petersburg, Russia, and at Butler University, where he received his BFA in Dance Performance. He has danced for Ballet Arkansas, Indianapolis Opera, and American Cabaret Theatre, as well as other guest artist appearances. In addition to performing, he teaches dance at Indianapolis School of Ballet and Pilates at Mindful Movement Studio. Last summer he had the opportunity to study at the Martha Graham Center for Dance Education in NYC to deepen his knowledge of the Martha Graham Technique. This is Timothy's 7th DK season.

86

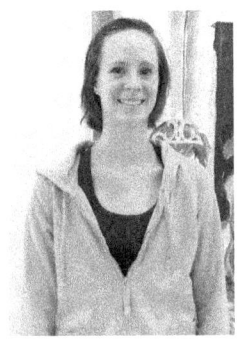

Mandy Milligan was raised in Sidney, Ohio and began dancing at a very early age at Sharon's School of Dance. She attended Interlochen Arts Academy, graduating with the honor of most improved student in 2010. She attended the University of Cincinnati's College Conservatory of Music where she received her BFA in Dance Performance. While at UC she was an apprentice with MamLuft&Co. Dance and also studied abroad at the Beijing Dance Academy in China. This is Mandy's first season as a DK trainee dancer.

Caitlin Negron began her dance training in her hometown of Fort Wayne, IN at Fort Wayne Ballet. She continued her studies at Southern Methodist University and graduated summa cum laude with degrees in Dance Performance and Anthropology. Other training includes the Martha Graham School, Thodos Dance

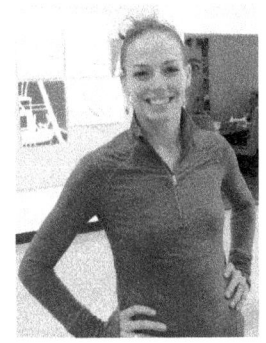

Company, American Ballet Theater and Richmond Ballet. She has attended workshops with Nina Wolly, 360 Dance Company, Alex Ketley and Garret-Moulton Productions. In 2008 Caitlin co-founded and currently serves as the executive director of The Indy Convergence, a pop-up arts residency program for professional artists held annually in Indianapolis, Toronto, and Jacmel, Haiti. She is also a BASI certified Pilates teacher and teaches classes throughout Indianapolis. This is Caitlin's 7th DK season.

Missy Trulock began gymnastics training at age three, continuing for 13 years as a competitive gymnast. She also studied modern dance, ballet and jazz at Rhythm Nations Studio in Euless, TX. Missy is a graduate of the Indiana University Modern Dance program. She recently attended the Martha Graham summer Dance intensive in New York. Through colorguard, she has performed with top organizations such as the Phantom Regiment Drum and Bugle Corps and Zydeco Color Guard. Missy 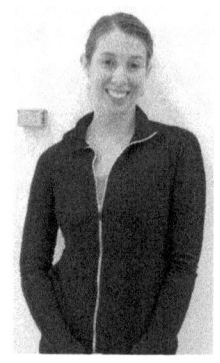 also has choreographed movement and dance for the marching field for many programs in Texas, Oklahoma, Arkansas, Indiana, and a Junior Corps in Quiberon, France. This is Missy's second DK season as an apprentice.

Noah Trulock began his performing career with the Cavaliers drum and bugle corps at age 15. He toured for several seasons with the Cavaliers and Phantom Regiment performing in featured roles across the country. Noah studied dance at Indiana University through the contemporary dance program where he 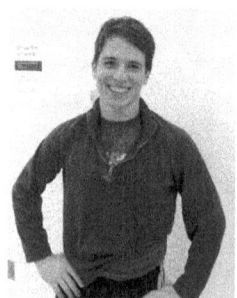 worked with several professional artists, including Connie Dinopoli, Liz Lerman, Nai-Ni Chen, David Parsons, Ben Munisteri, and David Hochoy. He recently attended the Martha Graham summer dance intensive in New York. This is Noah's 4th DK season.

Cover Artist Biography

Andrea Boucher is currently earning her MFA in the Butler University Creative Writing program. After building a career in the corporate world as an editor and technical writer for various companies, she decided to do what she really wanted in life, which is to be a literary nonfiction writer who moonlights as a book designer. In addition to this anthology, she also designed *I Remember: Indianapolis Youth Write about Their Lives* and *The Central and Southern Indiana 2014 Scholastic Art & Writing Awards.*

Editor Biographies

Barbara Shoup is the author eight novels, including four for young adults, and the co-author of *Novel Ideas: Contemporary Authors Share the Creative Process.* She is the Executive Director of the Indiana Writers Center. Her most recent novel, *Looking for Jack Kerouac,* was published by Lacewing Books in 2014.

Michael Baumann is a writer, a performer, and a teaching associate earning a Master of Arts in Rhetoric and Composition at Ohio University. He has edited five anthologies for public memoir writing projects with the Indiana Writers Center.

Acknowledgements

The Indiana Writers Center gratefully acknowledges the support of these individuals and organizations:

Editors
Michael Baumann
Andrea Boucher
Barbara Shoup

Cover Design
Andrea Boucher

Cover Photo
Heinz H. Weissenstein

Program Committee
Liberty Harris, Dance Kaleidoscope
Lisa Freeman, JCC
Lori Moss, Reuben Center
Sandy Reiberg, Dance Kaleidoscope
Lev Rothenberg, JCC
Barbara Shoup, Indiana Writers Center
Lynn Webster, Dance Kaleidoscope
Cindy Wides, Reuben Center

Individual Donors
Anonymous
Debra Horberg
Dwayne Isaacs
Michael Johnson
Sonja Kantor
Lori Schankerman
Harry Todd
Eleanor Vonnegut

Organizations
Albert and Sarah Reuben Senior and Community
Research Center
Dance Kaleidoscope
Health Foundation of Greater Indianapolis
JCC Indianapolis
Suzy Beeton Herring Memorial Dance Fund

Transcribers
Lisa Freeman
Bonnie Maurer
Linda Lee
Charr Skirven

www.ingramcontent.com/pod-product-compliance
Lightning Source LLC
Chambersburg PA
CBHW072157170526
45158CB00004BA/1681

* 9 7 8 0 9 8 4 9 5 0 1 5 7 *